Buddhism

The Art of Living A More Mindful Life

Introduction

We want to thank you and congratulate you for downloading the book, *"Buddhism: The Art of Living A More Mindful Life"*.

The importance of spirituality in this modern life is tantamount. We wake up every morning and **begin our quest for money, luxury, power** and what not. We live in air conditioned houses and stand in traffic. It would only be too easy to believe that we have everything we want, and that we feel content. However, each one of us knows that this is untrue.

We are stressed out about our careers, we have to strive to stay focused and loyal in our relationships, we are lonely even when we are in the midst of a crowd. We need sleeping pills to fall asleep. The future holds anxiety and the past is full of regret. And that's where it all begins... The **longing for peace and serenity**, the thirst for truth. We crave for balance. But how do we achieve this?

Through this book, we seek to **guide you in your journey to peace and mindfulness**. This text contains various teachings of Gautama Buddha – the one who taught the world about karma and mindfulness. He advocated several techniques for the attainment of the same. This book is a detailed and simplified account of Buddhist teachings and philosophies. Take a minute off from your busy life to invest in something truly valuable, and to find yourself. Find out how you can be fully present; without anxieties about the future or regrets about the past.

This text will help you **realize and explore different levels of your own being** and pave the way to the attainment of mental peace and bliss. In this busy world where stress and fatigue dominate a major part of our lives, it is important to set some time aside for spiritual pondering and self-realization. Practices like meditation help a great deal in our journey to bliss. They help us stay in touch with ourselves, help us to find happiness within ourselves and then to bring forth that happiness and spread it all around the world.

Thanks again for downloading this book, we know you will enjoy it!

Table of Contents

information is without contract or any type of guarantee assurance.

The trademarks that are used are without any consent, and the publication of the trademark is without permission or backing by the trademark owner. All trademarks and brands within this book are for clarifying purposes only and are the owned by the owners themselves, not affiliated with this document.

Chapter 1:
Buddhism

Buddhism is a religion that encompasses several traditions, beliefs and teachings. It mainly advocates "the middle path" which is the path between worldliness and extreme sacrifice. It is Gautama Buddha who developed this "middle path".

The world is full of religions that preach that selflessness and self sacrifice is the is the purpose of life. However, Buddha had different views. He believed that the purpose of life lies in developing the ability to be fully present and fully conscious. He called this state "mindfulness". Another intriguing feature of Buddhism is that it does not assert the existence of a higher power. The Buddhists do not worship deities or engage in idoization.

Buddhism originated around 2500 years ago. Today, this religion has over 300 million followers, known as Buddhists. Buddhism is widely accepted in Nepal, Tibet, China and other Southeast Asian countries. Over the years, Buddhism has diversified into several schools of thought. The most prominent of these are Theravada, Mahayana and Vyasayana. This religion believes in the doctrine of karma and rebirth. However, it does not believe in the existence of "the soul". Buddha asserted that everything in life is temporary.

The word Buddhism is derived from the Sanskrit word "Budhi" which means "to awaken". Buddhism is more than just a religion, it is a way of life. It is a practice. The religion stresses that man must develop the ability to be aware of his thoughts and actions.

The main teachings of Buddhism are:

- To be mindful of ones thoughts and actions

- To live in adherence to moral principles

- To develop wisdom, balance and understanding

- To develop simplicity and humility

- To strive towards the attainment of nirvana

Buddhism advocates that man can find solutions to all his problems from within himself. In order to find these solutions one must pay attention to his inner self, listen to his inner voice and observe his own thoughts and actions.

Chapter 2:
From Prince Siddhartha to Gautama Buddha

Birth and Early Childhood

Gautama Buddha, fondly known as 'Sakyamuni' was born to the Sakya King Sudhodana and Queen Maya of the Kapilavasthu realm of Nepal. Gautama Buddha was born in a small village called Lumbini in Kapilavashthu. Legend has it that Queen Maya dreamt one night that a brilliant and beautiful white elephant descended from the heavens and entered her womb. This was interpreted as a sign preceding the birth of a great revolutionary emperor. Ancient tales claim that Queen Maya gave birth to Gautama in a forest without endurance of any pain and that he immediately walked and talked. It is said that the newborn took seven steps in each direction and declared that he was born to initiate a spiritual revolution in the world. However, this part of the legend is dismissed as a mere old wives tale by most researchers. The baby was named Siddhartha. Queen Maya passed away seven days after the birth of Buddha. Siddhartha was adopted by Queen Maya's sister, who was also married to the king. She was extremely devoted to the baby.

According to ancient legends, the baby Prince Gautama was visited by Asita, a renowned ascetic of the time. The sage had heard of the birth of prince Gautama. King Suddhodana was overwhelmed by the fact that a great sage like Asita should take interest in his son. The King requested the sage to bless his son. However, when the sage bent over to bless the baby, the baby's feet turned upwards and rested on the sage's head. The wise sage easily realized that the little prince before him was no ordinary baby; that this was a true spiritual emperor. Sage Asita recognized in the baby, the thirty-two true signs of someone who would enter into great spiritual vocation. It is said that the sage smiled at the prince for a while and then became sad. King Sudhodana, who couldn't decipher the meaning of this asked the wise sage what was wrong. The sage responded saying that he was happy because the Prince would become an enlightened one, but he was sad because the sage's time to depart the world had arrived just when the Prince was born. The sage predicted that Siddhartha would renounce worldliness and attain knowledge that no man had attained before, that he would attain knowledge powerful enough to destroy the cycles of birth and death. The ascetic predicted two possibilities. He professed that the Prince would become either a universal monarch or an ascetic of the highest wisdom. The king questioned further to find out what would lead the prince towards the life of an ascetic. The sage responded saying that the same would happen if the prince cast eyes on four omens namely, an old man, a sick man, a corpse and a monk. King Sudhodana assumed that the prince was more likely to become a supreme emperor. However, he did not take Sage Asita's prophecy lightly and did everything within his power to ensure that the young prince shall not witness any one of these four sights. Siddhartha was raised in great luxury. The king filled the palace and its grounds with every object of luxury and pleasure, with the intention of luring the young prince into worldliness. He ensured that prince did not leave the palace.

Youth and Renunciation

According to the legends, Siddhartha grew up to be a youth of celestial beauty and sharp intelligence. He learned the sciences relevant to his tribe in a small amount of time. Siddhartha's extra ordinary intelligence and absolute wisdom started to disturb the king. The king could see possibilities of the Prince wanting to renounce the throne. With an intention to avoid this, the King surrounded the young prince with luxury and riches. He took several efforts to keep the prince entertained and occupied within the palace grounds in order to prevent the prince from leaving. When the prince turned sixteen, the king found the most beautiful maiden of the land and got her married to the prince. Her name was Yashodara. The king built three palaces suitable for three seasons for the young couple. He surrounded the prince with music, wealth and every other object of pleasure practically conceivable. The King made arrangements with the wise scholars of the palace to educate the Prince. Hence Siddhartha learnt the scriptures and other holy material. However, though Siddhartha was surrounded by luxury, he was never at peace. He started realising that luxury and royalty didn't make him feel whole.

With every passing day his spiritual longing grew stronger and his inner voice grew louder. As days passed Siddhartha grew less interested in the worldly luxuries of the palace. When he could no longer ignore his conscience Siddhartha confronted the king of this matter. The King was extremely disturbed by this confrontation. He increased the guard around the palace to ensure that Siddhartha did not leave the palace grounds.

The birth of Siddhartha's first and only son gave him some relief. He named his son Rahula, meaning 'rope'. Researchers believe that this name signifies the feeling of bondage and oppression that Siddhartha was experiencing at that point of time. It is said that one night, Siddhartha had a dream where he saw himself renouncing the throne and putting on the orange robes of an ascetic. All of this is symbolic of Siddhartha's inability to be immersed in worldliness even when surrounded by it. One day the young prince requested his charioteer to take him out of the palace grounds on an excursion. When King Sudhodana heard of this, he immediately ordered that the kingdom be cleaned and decorated and that all signs of old age, decease and death be removed. Thus the streets were cleaned and adorned with beautiful ornaments. They were cleared of the old, the sick and the dead. However, when Prince Siddhartha ventured out he still encountered all four of the forbidden sights. He became extremely disturbed by the sights of old age, death and sickness. He became intrigued by the peaceful disposition of the ascetic.

As predicted by Sage Asita, Prince Siddhartha made up his mind to renounce the throne. One night, while everyone else slept, Prince Siddhartha left the palace leaving behind every element of luxury, his wife and son, his father and his palace. Thus, he began the journey to nirvana. He went to a place near Bodh Gaya and practiced meditation. He meditated for years under the Bodhi tree. It is said that the powerful demon, Devaputra Mara made several attempts to break Siddhartha's meditation. However, Siddhartha's concentration only grew stronger and deeper.

With the intensity of his concentration and perseverance, Siddhartha unveiled the final shreds of ignorance from his mind and emerged as 'Buddha, the Enlightened One'.

Chapter 3:
Karma, The Law of Cause and Effect

The doctrine of karma was prevalent even before the advent of Buddhism as Hinduism is centred on this doctrine. In simple words, Karma is the law of cause and effect. According to the Hindu philosophy, every action has a corresponding reaction. Good and bad deeds result in good and bad effects respectively. The effect of karma last for lifetimes and one obtains salvation or 'moksha' when the effect of karma is destroyed. Hence, karma is the cause of rebirth. To be freed of the cycles of birth and death, one must undertake meditation and other spiritual practices. Buddha explained the doctrine of karma from all angles. He taught the world about karma and its effects. The explanation for the doctrine of karma as per Buddhism is not very different from that given by Hinduism. Buddhism asserts that one is responsible for his or her actions and that actions give rise to results. Like the Hindus, the Buddhists also believe that karma determines the fate of a person. According to Buddhism, karma is the real cause for inequality in mankind. It is because of karma that some people are born rich and some poor, some people are born beautiful and others ugly. Karma is the invisible cause for this inequality. However, not all the results one faces is a consequence of actions in the present life. Some of these may be traced to a recent or remote past life.

Buddha spoke of karma as thus:

"All living beings have actions as their own, their inheritance, their congenital cause, their kinsmen, and their refuge. It is karma that differentiates beings into low and high states."

Buddha further explained that karmic results that we inherited in our past lives have more effect on our present lives than our present heredity, circumstances and conditions. For instance, Buddha was born like every other normal person, but he was even raised in royal luxury. However, in the end, he renounced every element of luxury in his life and transformed into the sage of sages. One would no longer link him to the lineage of royal kings but to the lineage of ascetics. Hence Buddha became who he is because of his karma. The same is the case with every other human being. One's action decides his destiny. Who you will become is completely dependent on how you choose to act. The choices we make, makes us who we are far more than our heritage, talents and abilities. Prince Siddhartha chose to be Gautama Buddha. This was an unusual and extraordinary choice. Such is the power of our actions. It becomes easy to conclude that karmic actions can not only affect the temperamental conditions in our lives, but also invalidate the absolute conditions like our heritage and our genetic characteristics. Hence according to Buddhism, our mental, physical and temperamental aspects are the result of our actions.

However, Buddhism does not assert that everything that happens in our lives is due to karma. Buddha did not advocate that every aspect of a persons life is ruled by karma. If that were the case, then, there would be no point in living life. If all our acts were predetermined and if our future was already predesigned, then we would be mere puppets being controlled by a puppeteer. Buddha did not believe that our fates are pre-designed. He advocated that actions give rise to results. Buddha believed in the doctrine of free will. He believed strongly that man had the freedom to make his own decisions.

According to Buddhism there are five orders that influence our lives and karma is only one among them. The five orders of Buddhism are:

1. **Utu Niyama**: This "Niyama" or 'order' speaks of the inorganic, physical aspects of the world we live in. It explains why we have four seasons, why the winds change direction, why the sun rises and sets etc.

2. **Bina Niyama**: This relates to the organic physical conditions existent in our world like the timely germination of seeds, timely growth and ageing of beings, etc.

3. **Karma Niyama**: This is the order of cause and effect. This Niyama states that good actions give rise to good results and bad actions give rise to bad results. This is natural, absolute and inevitable.

4. **Dhamma Niyama**: This is the order of spirituality and other natural phenomenon and includes the behaviour of gravitation, the doctrine of birth and rebirth, etc.

5. **Citta Niyama**: This is the order of the mind and other psychological factors like consciousness, conscience, mindfulness, telepathy, etc.

The Utu Niyama and the Bina Niyama occur mechanically. They relate to man's physical surroundings and conditions. The Dhamma Niyama is also more or less physical. The Karma Niyama and the Citta Niyama however are psychological and karmic. Buddhism believes that the ability to control ones mind is the most powerful skill and that the attainment of this skill will aid in the destruction of karma. According to

Buddhism, the fruit of karma is called "vipaka". Vipaka is experienced as happiness or unhappiness. When the vipaka is good, it is experienced in the form of prosperity, happiness, good health, longevity and mental peace. This advantageous vipaka is also called "Anisama". When vipaka is bad it is experienced in form of distress, bad health, poverty, etc and this state is called "Adinaya".

However, the religion does not regard Anisama and Adinaya as rewards and punishments granted by a higher power. They do not believe in a higher power. They simple view vipaka as results of actions, as the effect of a cause and not as a post-mortem justice procedure. The main cause of the cycles of birth and death, as per Buddhism is "Avijja" or 'ignorance'.

The religion further believed that karma gives rise to "Gati Sampatti" or favourable birth, and "Vipatti" or an unfavourable birth. Gati Sampatti and Vipatti have a great influence in the choices we make in our present lives. "Upadhi sampattil" or good appearance, and "Upadhi Vipatti" or bad appearance are other factors that influence karma. For instance, if a person is born into a well to do family, in a happy state, it becomes easier for him to focus on good actions and results. On the other hand if a person is born into a poor family without any good looks, then it becomes more difficult for them to focus on karma and vipaka. However, this does not mean that a mans life is based purely on karmic results. It is sometimes seen that people who are rich and good looking live an unhappy life and people who are poor live content lives.

The story of Angulimala is of prime importance while explaining the law of karma. The story follows as thus:

Angulimala was a brilliant student. He was every teacher's favourite. Other students studying in the same university as

Angulimala grew jealous of him. They devised several schemes to get the teachers to hate Angulimala and succeeded in accomplishing their goal. The teachers, who wanted to trouble Angulimala ordered that he make a honorarium with a thousand human fingers. Aggravated and sad, Angulimala decided that he will not give up easily and that he will make the honararium. So he started killing people and chopping off their little finger. One day Buddha happened to see Angulimala. Angulimala jumped at Buddha for his finger as well. However, Buddha was not the least bit scared or disturbed. This reaction caught Angulimala by surprise. Buddha used this opportunity to speak to Angulimala. He advised Angulimala to stop what he was doing. Buddha spoke to him about the law of Karma. The enlightened one's wise words had tremendous impact on the serial killer. Angulimala immediately resolved to never hurt another human being ever again. He then joined the Buddhist monastery and lived the rest of his life like an ascetic.

Like Hinduism, Buddhism too regards karma as the Doctrine of cause and effect. The religion asserts that one shall eat the consequences of his own actions. As mentioned before, Buddhism doesn't believe that the results of karma are rewards or punishments granted by a superior being. They simply see it as positive and negative consequences of actions.

Chapter 4:
Different Traditions of Buddhism

Buddhism spread like wild fire across Asia. China, Bangladesh, Thailand, Nepal and other south East Asian countries embraced the religion whole heartedly. Consequentially, several schools of the religion started evolving and developing. Each school of Buddhism had its own traditions, practices and systems. However the crux and philosophy of the religion were the same with regard to all these schools. Of course there were minor differences in their beliefs, but the essence of their teachings remained the same. To fully understand Buddhism, it becomes important to study the different schools of Buddhism. They are Theravada, Vipasana, Mahayana, Zen, Nichiren and Pure Land Traditions. Given below is a detailed account on each of these schools of thought.

1. Theravada

Theravada, also known as "the doctrine of elders" is recognized as the oldest and most authentic school of Buddhism. This school was developed by the earliest followers of Buddha. They were part of his monastery during the Buddhas lifetime. "Pali Canon" is accepted by the Theravada Buddhists as the real teachings of Buddhism. The word "Pali" referers to the language in which Buddha taught and the word "canon" means teachings or suttas. This school of Buddhism is prevalent mainly in Sri Lanka, Combodia, Burma and Thailand. According to the Theravadans, a true Buddhist is one who is an "arhat" or "arhaant" which means "the deserving one". Hence it becomes right to say that the Theravadans believed that only a person who truly followed the religion and practiced it wholeheartedly deserved to be a Buddhist.

They assert that an ideal Buddhist is one who strives for Nirvana or Salvation. While the Theravadans who strive for salvation look up to Buddha as a spiritual master, they do not focus on worship of Buddha, but on following the teachings and methods for attainment of salvation as laid down by him. Theravadans believe that true arhants are monks who are able to withdraw from the world and be fully immersed in attaining their goal of nirvana. The Theravada school of Buddhism is known by several names. The oldest name for this school of thought is "Dhamma Vinaya", which means "the doctrine and discipline". Today, this school of thought has over 100 million followers worldwide and is slowly becoming popular in Europe and America.

Pali is the language of the Theravadans. This is a derivation of the Mahadi language that was spoken during the Buddha's life time. All of the Buddhas teachings and verses were in this language. Buddha's close followers had the practice of recording his sermons. Shortly after the Buddha left his physical form to attain pari nirvana, his followers gathered together to recite his teachings. Each of these recitals began with the phrase "Evam me sutam" which translates into "thus I have heard". All these sermons become the content of the Pali Canon which is the scripture of the Theravadans. The principle practices in the Theravada system include not only the study of the Pali Canon but also the practice of meditation.

The eight fold path and the four noble truths are the main teachings of Theravada Buddhism. It is to be noted that though the Theravadans follow the Buddhas teachings and pay homage to him, they do not worship gods or Bodhisatvas. Most Theravadans choose to be forest monks.

2. Vipasana

Vipasana is a form of Buddhism followed by westerners who were trained in countries like Thailand, Burma etc. They took the religion to the west. Vipasana is mainly meditation oriented. This meditation technique was discovered by the Buddha and taught by him. This technique focuses on finding ones self within ones self. It requires dedicated and relentless practice. This system advocates that man's problems are born in man's mind and not in the external world. So the solutions to these problems also exist inside man's mind. One only has look into himself to find answers to his questions. Constant practice of Vipasana meditation helps sharpen the mind and intellect. It helps one develop the ability to see things in their true and absolute form. The vipasana meditation has different stages. They are as follows:

- In the first stage the meditator observes his mind and body. He explores his thoughts and pays attention to his emotions. He observes each of these aspects carefully.

- The second stage takes place when the meditator realizes that his thoughts and emotions are temporary. In this stage thoughts and emotions disappear and it becomes easier for the meditator to focus.

- In the third stage the meditator tries to get rid of the joy within him. The only emotion left within him is peace.

- The fourth stage is characterized by pure mindfulness. At this stage the meditator becomes fully conscious. He is able to perceive that everything in this life is temporary and starts craving for freedom. He realises that everything is dynamic and changing.

Hence, Vipasana meditation, also known as "insight meditation" cuts through mind and matter and reveals to the meditator, the truth about life. It allows one to differentiate between the temporary and the permanent, the vague and the absolute. The vipasana meditation is becoming increasingly popular in this contemporary world. Several Buddhists offer dedicated classes and coaching for this meditation. Insight meditation is not an escape from reality but the confrontation of the same. It focuses on attainment of mindfulness through concentration. The proper name for insight meditation is "Vipasana Bhavana". It focuses on the development of mindfulness. The meditation requires extreme persistence and concentration. Mindfulness is achieved through observation. The vipasana meditation often considers objects relating to worldliness as soap bubbles. In order for the bubble to be born, one will have to blow it. Once someone blows a bubble it floats into the air. We are able to see it, we are sure it exists. In a while the bubble burst in front of our own eyes. According to Vipasana such is the nature of our thoughts and other worldly objects.

In Vipasana, meditators observe each thought and emotion, they see it being born, they witness its existence and then they watch it die before their eyes. This practice helps one to realize that everything that has a birth has a death as well, that nothing lasts forever or is permanent. The practice of Vipasanna meditation involves observation of five senses, namely, sight, hearing, smell, touch and taste. Meditators seek to realize that everything in life is temporary through this meditation.

3. Mahayana

Mahayana Buddhism is another school of Buddhism that follows the Pali Canon. This school of thought is popular mainly in Japan, Mongolia, Tibet and other North Asian countries. They engage in the study of several 'sutas' and ' sutras'. Practitioners of this school of thought, seek to become enlightened ones or 'bodhisatvas'. They then focus on assisting others in obtaining enlightenment. It is said that they purposely try to delay the attainment of nirvana to be able to help others. Mahayana Buddhists have religious systems and traditions. They engage in worship and rituals. They pay homage to celestial beings and employ religious equipment. Mahayana Buddhism evolved out of the popular Mahayana movement that took place over 2000 years ago. Several traditions and practices evolved as a part of this movement. The Mahayana movement was known by the name "great vehicle". The Mahayana Buddhism rose from the Mahasanghikas. They were the earliest followers of the Mahayana system.

The system grew extremely popular. They adopted monastic practices and rituals.

They believe that true Buddhists are related to the world only by external means. This form of Buddhism is divided into two sects:

- **Madhyamika**: This sect, as the name suggests, follows the middle path. Followers of this religion neither believe that everything in the world is real, nor that everything is unreal, they do not believe that every single object in the world is temporary but they also don't believe that everything is permanent.

- **Yogcara**: This is another important sect of the Mahayana school of Buddhism. It is called Yogcara because it focuses on attainment of bodha through the practise of yoga. It lays down ten stages of spiritual attainment to reach the final stage of bodha.

The Mahayana School also has other subdivisions. The most important of these are listed below:

- **Zen**: This school of Mahayana Buddhism was born in China. Today it is popular in Japan, Korea and Vietnam. This school advocates relentless meditation, observation and analysis of Buddhist literature and application of Buddhist principles in daily life, especially for the sake of others. This school does not believe that just knowing the Buddhist literature and laws makes one a Buddhist. They follow a special type of meditative practice called the Zazen. People practice Zazen in groups in meditative halls called Zendo. The steps to do Zazen have been elaborated below:

    a) The meditator places a low, flat mat known as Zabuton, on the floor.

    b) He then bows to the seat and his fellow meditators.

    c) He then closes his eyes and immerses himself in deep meditation when he hears the sound of the bell announcing the time to start mediating.

d) He continues to meditate till he hears the sound of the bell announcing the time to wind up the meditation.

The main practices of of the Zen school of thought include:

a. Observation of breathing patterns and thoughts.

b. Observation and exploration of one's mind.

c. Concentration to attain mindfulness.

d. Chanting of sutras and suttas.

- **Nichiren**: This school of Mahayana Buddhism is popularly known as the New Lotus school of Buddhism. The founder of this school was Nichiren. This school follows the crux of Buddhist teachings. They believe in reverence to the Buddhist sutras.

    a) **Pure land traditions**: This school, believes in worship of the Buddha. They believe that chanting the name of the Buddha will lead them to a place of pure happiness and that everything in this paradise will help them attain moksha.

    b) **Vajrayana**: This school of Buddhism is also known as the "Diamond Vehicle". It is known by several other names such as Mantrayana and Tantrayana. They believe in spiritual and ritualistic practices. This school of Mahayana Buddhism uses tantric techniques to attain bodha. They believe in the use of energy as a means to attain salvation. This is an extremely popular school of Buddhism.

Though Buddhism has several schools of thought, the essence of their teachings is the same. Furthermore, it is important to note that all these schools co-exist in peace.

Chapter 5:
Teachings of the Maha Buddha

After the Buddha attained enlightenment he decided to share his wisdom with the world. He attracted a lot of followers. While a lot of people today view the teachings of the Buddha as pessimistic, one who truly understands the religion will have no trouble in realizing that they are not. Buddha's teachings are solutions to problems we face today.

They show us how to find happiness and peace. The main quality of the Buddha's teachings is their utter simplicity. Buddha's teachings guide us in our journey to mindfulness. They help put an end to our sorrows and sufferings. His teachings are sensible, practical and logical. The main teachings of Buddha include:

1. **The three universal truths**

2. **The four Nobel truths**

3. **The eight fold path**

4. **The five percepts**

For better understanding of the Buddhist religion and Buddha's teachings, each of the above mentioned elements are explained in detail:

1. The Three Universal Truths

The three universal truths lay down the foundation for Buddhist teachings. These truths explain the nature of the universe. The three universal truths are known by the names Annica, Dukha and Anatta.

- **Annica**: This truth says that nothing in this universe is constant. Every single element in the universe is changing and dynamic. Everything from the tiny grain of sand to the vast mountains touching the sky are changing day by day. Sometimes, these changes are so minor that we do not notice them, but whether we notice or not, they keep happening. Buddha asserted that no element in the universe rests. Everything is constantly changing from one form to another.

- **Dukha**: The second universal truth says that suffering and sadness are inevitable in life. This does not just refer to pain or disdain but also to simpler aspects of suffering like discomfort, anger, fatigue etc. No one can escape suffering. If one lives life expecting to be happy all the time, he is bound to be disappointed. Happiness and sadness are like two sides of the same coin.

- **Anatta**: The third universal truth lays down that there is no such elect called "soul". A human being is basically his body, his mind, his thoughts, his feelings and his emotions. There is no part of him that may be carried on to a next life except the result of karma. Nothing in the world is eternal.

2. The Four Nobel Truths

The four Nobel Truths are important elements in Buddhist teachings. They explain the aspect of suffering, details on how suffering is caused and how it can be overcome. The four Nobel Truths are:

- **Sarvam Dukham**

- **Dukha Samuday**

- **Dukha Nirodhey**

- **Dukha Nirodha Gamini Pratipala**

The concept of suffering is illustrated in the Buddhist scriptures by a popular story. The story follows as thus:

One day a woman lost her first born child. The distressed woman wandered the streets, carrying her child in her arms, begging the people on the street to bring her child back to life. Some of the villagers took the woman to the Buddha. The Buddha listened to the woman's request and told her that he will bring the child back to life if she gives him a hand-full of mustard seeds. The Buddha specifically said that the mustard seeds must be brought from a family that has not been affected by death. Overwhelmed at the chance of having her dearest child back, the woman went around the village knocking on every door and asking if the family has been affected by death. She continued to do this until she knocked on every door at the village. However every house she had been to had been affected by death at some point of time. They had all lost grandparents, fathers, children, siblings or friends.

The woman went back to Buddha and said that she couldn't find a family that has never been affected by death. She bowed to him and told him that she now understood what he had intended to teach her from the beginning. Death and suffering are inevitable in life.

Buddha explained the concept of suffering through these four Nobel truths. Let us examine each of these in detail.

- **Sarvam dukham:** This Nobel truth explains that everything in the world is suffering and that no one escapes from suffering. We all experience suffering in different forms in our lives. It may be in the form of sickness, sadness or discomfort. We may have to be with people we dislike or do things we do not want to do. All this is suffering.

- **Dukha Samuday:** This Nobel truth lays down the cause of suffering. Buddha said that the cause of man's suffering is man himself. It is man's ignorance and craving that leads to suffering. When desires are not satisfied, there is suffering. If there are no desires, there is no suffering. Man is never satisfied with the basic amenities in life. He always wants more and he wants things that he does not have. When one need of his is satisfied, a new one arises. This, Buddha said, is the main cause of suffering.

- **Dukha Nirodhey:** This third Nobel truth lays down the ways to end suffering. The Buddha asserted that the only way to end suffering was by the elimination of desires. When one attains nirvana, he experiences a state of peace and bliss. Though this might sound easy, in reality, it is not easy at all. It takes a great deal of spiritual practice to be able to extinguish every desire that rises in the mind.

- **Dukha Nirodha Gamini Pratipala**: This Nobel truth lays down that the Eight Fold Path is the only path to end suffering.

Buddha asserted that suffering is inevitable and unavoidable. He explained the causes of suffering and went on to lay down steps to eliminate suffering from our lives. The Buddha quotes as thus:

"There is happiness in life,

Happiness is friendship,

Happiness of a family,

Happiness is a healthy body and mind,

But when one loses them,

There is suffering."

3. The Eight Fold Path

The symbol of Buddhism is a wheel with eight spokes. The eight spokes represent the eight steps of the Eightfold Path. The Buddha, at his first discourse at Deer Park spoke of the Eightfold path to salvation. For a better understanding of the Eightfold path, it has been detailed below:

I.   **Samma Ditthi**: This refers to complete and clear vision. However this does not pertain to physical vision but rather ones mental and spiritual vision. Sama Ditthi refers to the ability to see reality, ie; to see the world as it is. Only if one is able to see reality, will he be able to pursue it.

II.   **Samma Sankappa**: This refers to purity and righteousness in thoughts. This lies in the ability to filter ones thoughts and emotions and cleansing ones desires. It also relates to clarity in thoughts. Nirvana cannot be attained unless one tones and perfects his thoughts, aspirations and desires. A true Buddhist will only entertain good thoughts.

III. **Samma Vaka**: This refers to good, clear and genuine use of words. Words once uttered and arrows once sent cannot be taken back. Words have the strange ability to influence man and the people around him. Man must be conscious and careful about what he utters.

IV.   **Samma Kammanta**: This step refers to righteousness in action. Actions are the most important expressions of mankind. They truly depict what even words fail to convey. Hence purity in action is an important step in the attainment of Nirvana. A Buddhist must strive to control his actions and ensure that he acts purely, consciously and rightfully.

V.   **Samma Ajiva**: This refers to righteousness in ones way of life. Any person who aspires to attain nirvana must live in accordance with ethics and principles. One must live a life that is filled with justice, rightfulness, generosity and love.

VI.   **Samma Vayama**: This refers to right effort. One's efforts must be diligent and must be aimed at attainment of nirvana. Man must focus all his energy on attainment of the object of salvation.

One's efforts must also be directed towards helping others attain nirvana.

VII.   **Samma Sati**: This refers to right awareness and right mindfulness. In order to attain right mindfulness, one must focus on observing and cleansing his thoughts and emotions. He must develop the ability to concentrate on the attainment of nirvana.

VIII.   **Samma Samadhi**: We could attempt to define samadhi as concentration, awareness or consciousness but samadhi means much more than all those words put together. It refers to the establishment of oneself at the highest level of consciousness. It takes a great yogi to even attempt to reach this level. It is a state of mind. A person who has attained this state of mind has attained advanced spiritual progress. He is able to see reality and understand the universe.

Any person who wants to attain nirvana must follow the Eightfold path. The Eightfold fold path is of utmost importance to a Buddhist. It is among the most widely accepted teachings of the world.

4. The Five Percepts

The Five Percepts refer to five moral resolutions that every Buddhist must take. They are of utmost importance in Buddhism.

The Five Percepts have been listed below:

I.   **Panatipata veramani sikkapadam samadiyami**: This translates into "I pledge to abstain from destruction of any form of life." This refers to the moral obligation of respecting the principle of right to life. Every living organism in this world has as much right to live in this world as human beings do. One will be able to honour this pledge when he gardens kindness and compassion within himself and becomes empathetic to the suffering of other creatures.

II. **Adinnadana veramani sikkapadam**: This translates into "I pledge to abstain from taking that which was not given to me." In simple words, this means "I pledge not to steal." This percept shows respect for property owned by others. A true Buddhist, must strive to abstain from stealing or taking anything that does not rightfully belong to him. To steal from another is to steal from oneself. A person free of attachment will easily be able to abstain from stealing.

III. **Kamesu micchacara viramani sikkapadam samadiyami**: This translates into "I resolve to abstain from sexual misconduct". This involves refraining from any form of sexual aberration or adulteration. One must develop a high sense of morality and respect other's feelings and privileges.

IV. **Masuda viramani sikkapadam samadiyami**: This translates into "I pledge to refrain from falsehood." This involves a training from false practices like lying, cheating, fraud and other misconduct.

V.   **Suramerayamajjapamadatthana viramani sikkapadam samadiyami**: This translates into "I resolve to abstain from intoxicants that will cloud my mind and thoughts". At a social level it helps to prevent several social issues and accidents. At a personal level this helps develop a sound mind and clarity of thought.

Buddha's life in general is the best lesson he taught mankind. He personified love, kindness, righteousness, perseverance, intelligence and sacrifice. This is the reason why Buddhism is one among the most popular religions in the world.

Chapter 6:
Buddhist Practices

Buddhism, being a widely accepted religion has a number of practices. The popularity of this religion has led it to evolve into several sects and schools. Each of these schools have their own set of practices that are unique to them. However, there are certain practices like meditation and vegetarianism that are common to all Buddhists. The contemporary world has several centres teaching the practices of Buddhism as well. The main attracting trait of this religion is its sensibility. The practices are dynamic and they keep changing and evolving. The most popular Buddhist practices include:

1) Prayer

2) Meditation

3) Vegetarianism

4) Chanting

It becomes pertinent to study each of these practices in detail.

1) **Prayer**: The significance of prayer in Buddhism varies from school to school. Prayer is considered by many religions as the language of the soul. It is seen as the means of communication between man and his creator. However, most schools of Buddhism do not believe in a creators. Buddhists are primarily atheists. They do not usually engage in prayers or rituals. However, the Nichiren sect of Buddhism does believe is prayers. They also believe that honest prayers shall be answered. The steps to recite a Buddhist prayer is as follows:

a. Sit down and maintain a steady posture

b. Take a deep breath and close your eyes

c. Concentrate only on the prayer you are about to say

d. Repeat the mantra in your mind

e. Chant the three Jewel prayer of Buddha, Dharma and Sangha

f. Pray not only for your own happiness but also for the happiness of others

g. Pray before meals

h. Chant the meta prayer which is a special prayer advocated by the Buddha and it is said to be all encompassing

i. You could consider using Buddhist prayer beads to count your prayers. It is said that counting the beads helps concentrating and enables your body and mind to work in unison

j. Understand the significance of the bead chain which is made up of 108 beads

k. Chant a prayer for each individual bead

l. Ensure that your bead chain is kept in a sacred, clean and pure place.

2) **Meditation:** Meditation is an attempt to control the mind and senses. It is an effective spiritual practice accepted by religions all over the world. Meditation is the art generating inner peace from within oneself. In

Buddhism, meditation is the only way to curb and eventually extinguish desires. It is the most important step in the attainment of nirvana. "Apna sati" or mindfulness meditation and "Metta Bhavana" or loving kindness meditation are the two most prominent forms of Buddhist meditation. The four P's, namely place, problems, practice and posture are the main factors of Buddhist meditation. In order to begin, it is important to find an apt place, perhaps quiet where you are not likely to be interrupted. Second, sit in a comfortable posture. Fold your legs and keep your back straight. Now close your eyes and take deep breaths. You could also try sitting in a chair as long as you keep your back straight. Next comes the most important step. Pay close attention to the breaths you inhale and exhale. While you are paying attention to your breathing patterns observe the the rise and fall of the abdomen. After some time into meditation, you might experience certain problems and difficulties. This may be in the form of physical discomfort like itching, pain in the knees, restlessness, etc. Do not be distracted by this but keep focusing on your body. In the beginning you will be distracted by intruding thoughts that roam in your mind, thus diverting your attention from your breathing patterns. The best way to deal with this problem is to patiently and purposefully keep returning your attention to the breathing pattern. Constant practice in this manner will eventually weaken the strength and force of your thoughts and strengthen the intensity of your concentration. After some practice you will experience moments of deep mental calmness, bliss and mental peace.

The main meditation techniques have been stored in ancient Buddhist scriptures and have been transferred across generations and evolved through teacher-student relationships. Buddhists follow meditation as a method for attainment of nirvana. Buddhist meditation techniques spread their wings across continents and people all over the world have now accepted these teachings. Buddhism advocates a variety of meditation techniques that focus on developing mindfulness and attaining peace and tranquillity.

3. **Vegetarianism:** The common belief is that all Buddhists are vegetarians. but in reality some are not. The Buddhist practices and beliefs regarding vegetarianism vary from school to school. Whether a Buddhist should practice strict vegetarianism or not is still a grey area. It mainly depends on the perception of each person.

According to Tripitaka, Buddha did not advice his students to become vegetarians. He never forbade them from consumption of meat. In fact, Buddhist monks accepted all offerings whether vegetarian or non-vegetarian offered to them in their bowl. Most Buddhist monks are not vegetarians.

Considering that Buddha specifically pointed out what meat products Buddhists should refuse to eat, it could be assumed that Buddha permitted Buddhists to consume other meat products he didn't specifically prohibit. However, Buddhist monks would refuse to consume meat if they know that an animal was slaughtered specifically for them. However, they do not consider it wrong to consume the left over meat of an animal that was slaughtered to feed a family.

The counter argument to this is that if an animal were already killed for consumption by a family and not specifically slaughtered to be consumed by oneself, then it is very different situation. Buddhas perception on vegetarianism is quite vague.

It is to be noted that Buddha, as well as the monks and nuns who were his followers were wanderers who survived on the offerings they received. Buddhists did not have the practice of building monasteries and other permanent communities until a few years after Buddha attained pari nirvana. Buddhist monks survived not only on meat offered to them but also on cultivated vegetarian products. Most Buddhist monks avoid non vegetarian food to honour the first of the five Percepts of Buddhism.

For this reason, certain sects of Mahayana Buddhism in particular began to encourage vegetarianism. Most of the Mahayana scriptures, that include the Lankavatara, provide purposefully vegetarian teachings.

In today's modern world, the acceptance of vegetarianism in Buddhism differs from school to school. Followers of the Theravada school of Buddhism are strict vegetarians. They believe it is wrong to harm another being. The Vajrayana sect of Buddhism also promotes vegetarianism, though they do not hold it compulsory. Most followers of the Mahayana school of thought are also vegetarians.

4. **Chantings:** Chanting is a very common practice in all religions, and of great importance in Buddhism. However, the purpose for which the Buddhists chant is different from the purpose for which followers of other religions chant. The Buddhists do not chant for the purpose of offering prayers. They chant with the objective of increasing concentration and to increase focus. Buddhists

believe that repeating something in our mind helps us strengthen our believes and resolve.

However, there are certain sects of Buddhism that are interested in chanting as a form of prayer. The Tibetan form of Buddhism engages in worship and other ritualistic practices. The Buddhists use several articles like prayer beads, prayer wheels and prayer flags to intensify the power of their chantings.

Buddha has advocated several calculated praying and meditation techniques. Most of these techniques are even scientifically proven to provide peace and reduce anxiety and stress. These techniques require focus and concentration and must be practiced diligently.

Chapter 7:
Mindfulness

Mindfulness is the ability to be fully aware of ones self. One is aware of his thoughts, his actions, his feelings, his emotions, his breathing patterns, the changes happening in his body and so on. It means being fully involved in the present moment. It also means being able to observe without judging. Mindfulness is the most essential quality of a Buddhist. The Maha Buddha stressed the importance of this point over and over again in his sermons. He developed several steps to cultivate and maintain mindfulness. He taught his deciphers several meditation techniques and practices to attain mindfulness. Mindfulness is not an easy quality to cultivate. Its cultivation and development requires relentless practice and patience. Buddhists believe that one attains nirvana when he attains mindfulness.

Right mindfulness is part of the Eightfold path of Buddhism. It refers to the knowledge of a being's true nature and the nature of the world in which he lives. Mindfulness can be attained only through detachment and logic, thus mindfulness is the state of being fully conscious.   There are several ways to develop mindfulness:

Developing Mindfulness

Buddhism advocates several techniques to attain mindfulness. The mindfulness meditation and the love kindness form of meditation are the two most important of such steps. The steps to develop mindfulness have been detailed below:

- The first step to attaining mindfulness is being aware of your own breathing patterns. Notice your inhalation and exhalation. Feel the breath in your lungs.

- Concentrate on your breath and make sure you are not distracted. This will be difficult for beginners. Be aware of how long you inhaled and how long you exhaled. Also be aware of how long you held the air in your body.

- Now pay attention to your body, your posture and your movements, if any.

- When you pay attention to your body, you will start noticing different sensations like pain, discomfort, etc.

- Pay attention to each of these sensations. However don't let these sensations distract you from your objective. This will take constant practice.

- You are not to react to these discomforts, but to observe them carefully. The discomfort will disappear after a while.

As time progresses, the meditator will get closer to mindfulness. It is important to not rush and to not push yourself too much. Attainment of mindfulness must happen on its own. It cannot be forced. It will happen as naturally as a bud opening into a flower. When mindfulness is attained, the inner eye is opened and one will see the world in different light.

Maintaining Mindfulness

After attaining the state of mindfulness, the meditator must keep practicing to stay in that state of mind, to not stray away from the path to salvation. In order to stay in the state of mindfulness, the meditator must continue his meditative and spiritual practices. It must not be stopped once mindfulness is attained. According to the Buddhist principles, one becomes a true Buddhist only when he assists others to attain the same. Buddha compared the experience of attaining mindfulness to the strike of lightening; he said that it comes in a flash.

Mindfulness will make one more aware of who he truly is and with this realization comes joy and happiness. Maintaining mindfulness takes relentless effort, but the more you practice the easier it gets. People often get carried away by the feeling of joy experienced during the attainment of mindfulness. This might be a point of distraction. The meditator must not meditate with the intention of experiencing joy or happiness. He must rather focus on the process of meditation itself. When one observes his problems and feelings for an elongated period of time, one becomes aware that these problems and feelings are not real at all. Mindfulness must be watered and nourished just as a seedling is watered and nourished. It must be taken care of every day. With each passing day, the feeling of mindfulness will grow into a strong sturdy tree that has its roots deep in your mind. James Baraz spoke of mindfulness as thus:

"Mindfulness is simply being aware of what is happening right now without wishing it were different. Enjoying the present without holding on when it changes (which it will). Being with the unpleasant without fearing it will always be this way (which it won't)"

Chapter 8:
Why Meditate?

Once a man approached Buddha and asked him what he gained from meditation. His reply was this "Nothing, however, let me tell you what I lost – anger, anxiety, depression, insecurity, fear of old age and death". There is no better way to explain the power of meditation than this lucid statement made by the sage of sages. Meditation does not grant super powers, rather it enables one to see the truth. It brings forth peace of mind and tranquillity. Meditation removes the cloud of doubt from ones mind, allowing him to see clearly. It makes the meditator more aware and alert. Meditation is effective in handling stress and anxiety.

The most important benefits of meditation are:

Increase in concentration, ability to focus and alertness

Removal of stress, fatigue, anxiety, fear and tension

Buddhist meditation techniques are used to eliminate issues through concentration and observation

Meditation allows the meditator to find answers to questions and solutions to problems from within himself

Meditation allows the meditator to explore different levels of consciousness, thus bringing him closer to mindfulness

At a physical level, meditation increases cerebral capacity and boosts the functioning of physical organs, helps balance blood pressure and cholesterol levels

Meditation allows the meditator to find the inner peace that lies buried beneath all the chaos in his thoughts, feelings and desires

Buddha asserted that all evil arose from the mind. Cleansing the mind leads to cleansing the world of evil. He believed that a man is primarily his thoughts and emotions. Buddha said "it is better to conquer yourself, than to win a thousand battles. Then the victory is yours, and it cannot be taken from you." This victory can be attained only through meditation.

Chapter 9:
Effective Meditation Techniques

Meditation must be practiced effectively on a daily basis. For meditation to be effective, the mediator must be patient and he must fully understand the science of meditation. It is said that the process of meditation is similar to the process of a flower blooming. The mind opens its petals one by one as it passes through different levels of consciousness. Meditation offers many psychological and physical benefits to the mediator. At a spiritual level, meditation even has the power to extinguish the fires of karma and vipaka.

Buddhism advocates several meditation techniques. Among these, the most popular techniques are the mindfulness meditation technique and the love kindness meditation technique.

Mindfulness Meditation

Mindfulness meditation is a Buddhist meditation technique that focuses on attainment of mindfulness through concentration on breathing patterns and physical and mental sensations. When the meditator pays attention to himself, his body and his mind, he becomes more aware and more present. This paves way to mindfulness. The different steps to mindfulness meditation has been detailed below:

Focus on inhaling and exhaling though your nose

Observe the rise and fall of your abdominal area as you breathe

You could try counting your breaths in order to stay focused and alert

Do not force your mind to stop thinking. Allow thoughts to flow into your mind freely as they come; this is only natural for beginners

You will definitely experience discomforts like pain, restlessness and drowsiness. Instead of being distracted by them, pay attention to these sensations, observe them until they disappear

As days pass, increase the time period of your meditation – make sure this is done gradually

Love Kindness Meditation

This is a Buddhist meditation technique to nourish the feelings of love and kindness within the meditator. This format of meditation can be practiced only after the meditator has practiced mindfulness meditation. The steps involved in love kindness meditation has been detailed below:

While you're meditating, strive to increase the feeling of love and compassion for yourself, the people you love and for other fellow beings

The best way to accomplish this is to think about someone you love and respect while meditating

Pay attention to your body and your breath in patterns when you're meditating

Make sure you don't get lost in your thoughts, and that you stay aware through the process

Imagine yourself with the person you are considering

Focus on the emotion you feel towards the person you are considering

It is important to ensure that you focus on the feelings of love and kindness and not on the object of your meditation

Once the feeling in born in you, concentrate on increasing the feeling

Imagine projecting the feeling of this love and kindness across the four directions of the compass

In order to be successful in this, imagine four people you love in each of the four directions

Now concentrate on radiating this feeling of love and kindness from yourself to the entire world

The practice of this method of meditation will surely foster compassion within the meditator. Buddha often said that man eventually becomes what he

constantly thinks about. Thinking of love and compassion makes one loving, compassionate and kind. This is exactly what the world needs, a population

overflowing with compassion and kindness. This will put an end to all problems in the world like poverty, fraud and war. Being compassionate to one another and

to the other beings in the world (even the inanimate ones like trees and plants) will surely make the world a much better place to live in.

Chapter 10:
Mindful Meditation for Beginners

Meditation is a skill that every human being must develop. The ability to meditate is the ability to act consciously and with care. According to Swami Sivananda:

"Meditation is the dissolution of thoughts in eternal awareness or pure consciousness without objectification, knowing without thinking, merging finitude in infinity."

Attaining nirvana through meditation is like waking up after a million decades of sleep. It brings forth the light of wisdom in the dark tunnel of ignorance. The art

of meditation can be mastered only through constant practice. It might prove difficult for beginners. The following tips will be useful for novel meditators:

Choose to meditate in a place that is quiet, peaceful and clean. Your surroundings have immense power to influence your mind. Picking the right place to meditate will help a great deal.

Wear clothes that are comfortable and conducive to breathing freely. Wearing clothes that are too tight will hinder the free flow of your breath. This will reduce the effectiveness of meditation.

Do not try too hard in the beginning. The art of meditation can be learned only gradually. Rushing the learning process will only take you further away from your goal.

Close your eyes and take full and deep breaths. This increases oxygen supply to your brain, thus making you more conscious.

Focus on your breathing patterns. Observe the length of time taken for each breath. Feel the breath in your lungs. Observe the movement happening in your body with each breath.

Observe every thought that wanders into your mind. Observe every emotion, every feeling in your mind. Observe as thoughts start, grow and die in your mind.

All the above mentioned steps will enable the meditator to be fully present and wholly aware. Following these steps will bring the meditator one step closer to their goal.

Chapter 11:
Incorporating Buddhism in
Your Daily Life

"Every morning, we are born again. What we do today is what matters the most". This famous quote by Buddha signifies the importance of living each day mindfully. It is extremely important to incorporate values and principles into our daily lives. This ensures peace and tranquility in the world. Living mindfully each day will not be easy in the beginning. You may feel the need to give up. However, living mindfully is the only way to solve issues we face in our daily lives. Man must learn to be at peace with the fact that everything in this world keeps changing with time. He must understand that expecting something to last forever will only bring forth distress.

Pursuit of Happiness

Life is often seen as the pursuit of happiness. The yearning for happiness is a natural instinct. Nobody wants to be unhappy. When a person is happy, he wants the feeling to last forever. He does everything within his capacity to maintain it. When a person is unhappy, he tries to push the feeling away. He either broods about it or thinks of ways to forget the factor that's making him unhappy. Every other desire of a human being is incidental and ancillary to the desire for happiness. Man seeks money, wealth, company and other aspects to attain happiness. However, Buddha said "there is no path to happiness, happiness is the path itself".

Letting Go of Clinging

When we are happy or when we have something we like, we have the tendency to want to make it last forever. We do not want to accept that the world is dynamic. We do not want to accept change. Similarly, when we are facing something negative, we are scared that it will last forever. A true Buddhist would know otherwise.

Don't Take It Personally

"Why did this happen to me?" This is a question we ask ourselves and the people around us when things do not go our way. We are demanding explanations for why something negative has happened to us. The only practical answer is that negativity and misfortune may be bestowed on anybody. There is no need to take this personally. Instead, realize that the suffering is only temporary and move on in life.

Opening to Love

"For hate is never conquered by hate. Hate is conquered by love. This is an eternal law." This is a famous quote by Buddha who did conquer the world with his love for humanity and other beings.

Buddha, in his sermons, emphasised the importance of love. He said that the best and most important kind of love, is one's love for oneself. Only when one loves oneself, will they be able to love another. This is very true. You can only share what you already have. It is not possible to share something you do not possess. If a man does not love himself, then there is no love inside him. He will not be able to love others. We are often distressed and upset about "not being loved". Sometimes people are sad because the person from whom they crave love does not love them back enough. This causes suffering. The sting of love can be the worst and most unbearable pain in the world. This is why people are often scared to open up to love or to expect love. So then if love has the ability to hurt us so much, then why does Buddha ask us to be open to love? Perhaps the reason is that Buddha's definition of love is different from ours, or perhaps because he understands the depth of this emotion far more than we do. When you love someone and expect them to love you back the same way, such love can no longer be called selfless. If love isn't selfless, it isn't love at all. It is merely attachment. It is attachment that causes pain and not love. The Bible says that love is patient, kind, selfless and all forgiving. Being able to love that way is being able to put an end to a lot of suffering that we endure.

Buddha advocated the Love Kindness meditation to help people develop this ability. This meditation focuses on nourishing the feelings of love and compassion in your heart. The Buddha asked his disciples to meditate on someone they love. However, he asked them to ensure that their focus must be on the emotion of love and not on the person they are thinking of. Men must strive to foster the feeling of compassion within them. They must feel for other fellow beings. Man must realize that the whole world is his family, and that every other being deserves to be loved.

Buddha said that hate is not an answer to anything. Hate, greed and ignorance are the main reasons for suffering in this world. Man must develop the ability to love and take care of another as much as he loves himself. This will ensure peaceful co-existence between beings. Love is the most powerful force in the world. It has the ability to change the reason for one's existence, to redefine every aspect about him once and for all. Only the rays of love can warm a cold soul or heal a broken heart.

Love has the power to open the inner eye and to fill one with bliss and peace. However, one must have the insight to differentiate between love and attachment. Being able to make this distinction will change one's life forever.

Anger Management

One day a young boy had fight with his mother. He said things that he didn't mean because of his anger. This left his mother deeply wounded. The young boy's father, who had listened to the conversation between the mother and son called

the boy aside and walked him to the wooden fence guarding their home. He asked the boy to not speak when he is angry. The father then handed him a bag of nails

and a hammer and told him to hammer a nail into the fence whenever he was angry. The son did as he was told. After a few days, the boy ran out of nails. When

the young boy confronted his father of this fact, the father asked the boy to remove the nails one by one from the fence whenever he was angry. Once again,

the boy took his father's advice. Soon, all the nails were removed from the fence. The fence was a sad sight to look at. It was full of holes. The father said to the

young boy "son, this is what your anger can do to another person. It can damage them beyond repair. It can leave them broken. Even though you did remove the

nails that you had hammered from the fence, there is nothing you can do to fully mend the holes that they have left on the fence. This is the power of anger. You

might be able to apologize for your anger, but you will never be able to fully mend the victim of your anger."

Anger is a truly useless emotion. It is extremely harmful. It makes us blind and ignorant. We must do whatever it takes to ensure that this emotion is not entertained in our minds. Meditation is an effective technique of anger

management. When you are angry, choose not to react based on this emotion. Instead, concentrate on realizing that what you are experiencing is merely an

emotion. Observe the emotion in your mind. Soon you will feel it fading. By doing this on a regular basis, you are training your mind to ignore anger. The

hints given below will make the process of anger management easier for you. When you are angry, you should:

Leave the place immediately. It is best to not stay near the object of your anger. Leave the surroundings that ignited the anger within you and distract your mind.

Close your eyes and take deep breaths. Focus on your breathing. This will increase oxygen supply to your brain and help clam your mind.

Drink a glass of water. Drinking water will help a great deal in calming down. Calming down will help you focus better.

Look at the mirror. It is said that looking at a mirror when you are angry might make you laugh. While this might not be true for everyone, looking at the mirror will help you distract yourself. It will give you a view of your angry self.

Practice meditation on a constant basis. While meditating, think of positive traits like love, happiness, peace and bliss. Do not think of anger while meditating.

Anger is an extremely negative emotion. Only through conscious effort will you be able to eliminate it from your life.

Freedom From Fear

Buddha said "The whole secret of existence is to have no fear. Never fear what will become of you, and depend on no one. Only the moment you reject all help are you freed". We live in fear every day. Fear of death, fear of losing someone we love, fear of being poor, fear of being unsuccessful, etc. – these are only some of the fears we face every day. Living in fear is as good as being half alive. When you live in fear, you will not be able to be fully present or mindful. You will not be able to enjoy the many blessings in your life.

When we are in a good state, we are scared of losing it. When we are in a bad state, we fear it will last forever. The deepest reason for this is desire. It is our desire to be happy always and our desire to never be sad. However, this is an impossible goal to achieve. Happiness and sadness are like two sides of the same coin and are inevitable. Further, there is no way to put an end to suffering. Old age and death are also inevitable in life; there is absolutely no point in dreading them.

Compassionate Life

Compassion is the highest level of love and kindness. Buddhism stresses on the importance of developing love and kindness in one's life. Compassion also means 'empathy to other beings'. Man must feel sympathetic to other fellow beings. He must pay special attention to increase positive feelings like love and kindness within him. Similarly, man must take conscious effort to ensure that negative feelings are discarded from the mind. Man must have to ability to move beyond self-centeredness. It is easier to be compassionate when one realizes that his fellow beings also have wants and needs. They also want happiness and companionship.

While trying to develop compassion:

Start by being compassionate to your closest friends and family. It will be easier to do this if you're a beginner

Meditate on positive emotions every single day. This will strengthen the intensity of compassion

Develop slowly into a human being who is compassionate to every other fellow being, human or not

Compassion is one of the key traits in Buddhism. Buddhists strive to incorporate compassion into their daily lives. It is through compassion and love that we can truly make a change in the world.

Conclusion

We are honored by the fact that you took the time to read this book and educate yourself on the wonderful topic of Buddhism! We hope that this text helped you get **one step further in your journey** to mindfulness and conscious living. The ability to be fully aware and alert are skills that can be developed only with a lot of patience and practice.

It is important to invest your time and efforts in spiritual growth and evolution. It is through calmness, mindfulness and compassion that we can attain **true fulfillment in our lives**. It is through the knowledge of ancient tradition that we can discover the truth.

Buddha taught us that enlightenment is the only way to put an end to the cycles of birth and death. He portrayed this valuable lesson with his way of life, demonstrating the superiority of spirituality over materialism. He advocated steps to incorporate values and principles in our lives. Gautama Buddha asserted that **self mastery is the greatest worth**. Such self mastery can be accomplished only through meditation.

We hope that reading this book has brought you closer to yourself, and has **planted a seed of understanding** inside of you which will sprout into something beautiful. We are in a special time of awakening on earth, and we thank you for being a part of it!

Free Bonus eBook Access: 120 Powerful Quotes from Buddha

cure for the people

We really hope you enjoyed reading this book, and we want you to know that **we care about our community and the people in it**. That's why we began our collective called 'Cure For The People'. We love to publish lots of different content on various subjects from health to self-help, and much more. We want to open the minds and hearts of our readers, to spread awareness on important topics and have a good time doing it! However, we cannot do what we love to do... without you! Community is the most important part of this movement, and **we want you** to be a part of it!

We would love for you to interact with us and other like-minded individuals on our social media pages, as well as read more great articles and blogs on various related topics, and even get **free chapters from our other books** – all to be found on our website:

www.cure4people.com

You can also find more of our books and video trailers on Amazon which we know **you will LOVE**, by simply visiting our Amazon Author page:

www.amazon.com/author/cure4people

And one last, final thing...

Like we said earlier, community is the most important element required to continue spreading awesome life-changing information to the world – and so if we want people to discover and learn, we need people to trust us and our books! If you could be so kind and helpful, could you please leave us an **honest review** on our Amazon page for this book? We made it super easy and provided the link right here:

<u>www.amazon.com/review/create-review</u>

We give you our big thanks in advance for this super-awesome favor!

As a big 'THANK YOU' we have written a free bonus eBook, *just for you*. It's an eBook that has no availability or access anywhere but <u>right here</u>. As an even bigger bonus, when you download the free book, you will be subscribed to our newsletter which will continue to provide you **additional valuable content** on this particular subject. We want to continue supporting our readers by engaging with them after they read our books and this is the perfect way to stay connected.

So.. for the moment we have all been waiting for... We present to you... your free bonus ebook:

"120 Powerful Quotes from Buddha"

www.cure4people.com/buddhism-bonus-428

We hope you enjoy this free content, and we wish to continue our relationship through our newsletter, social media channels, website and blog.

Best Wishes from the Cure For The People family!

Made in the USA
Middletown, DE
15 May 2019